Birthday

Written by Jenny Feely
Illustrated by Mitch Vane

Tina had two candles on her birthday cake.

She blew them out
with one big blow.

Lee had five candles
on her birthday cake.

She blew them out
with one big blow.

Chen had ten candles on his birthday cake.

He blew them out
with one big blow.

Dad had forty candles on his birthday cake.

He blew them out
with one big blow.

Grandma had lots of candles on her birthday cake.

She blew and blew and blew

"Quick," she said.
"Help me blow them out."

We blew them out with one big blow!